The KEYS *to* SUCCESS *in* BUSINESS

Angela Preston

authorHOUSE®

AuthorHouse™ UK
1663 Liberty Drive
Bloomington, IN 47403 USA
www.authorhouse.co.uk
Phone: 0800.197.4150

Published by AuthorHouse 12/15/2016

ISBN: 978-1-5246-6543-2 (sc)
ISBN: 978-1-5246-6545-6 (hc)
ISBN: 978-1-5246-6544-9 (e)

Acknowledgements

Writing about the characteristics I believe are needed to become successful in Business is something I am very passionate about. I am reminded every day how important it is to keep educating and improving if we are to be the best version of ourselves and the only way to do that is to look for the best in your field of expertise.

Within the book I talk about different thought leaders, change makers and influencers and how their expertise and influence has changed the world when it comes to personal development. As well as those amazing individuals who have helped reshape the world and helped people to change their lives for the better, I met and was coached by a man I now consider a long term friend, Billal Jamil who is the CEO of The Public Speaking Academy and an executive coach, with his style of coaching and mentoring he challenged me to go to deeper levels to realise what can be achieved when you have an open mind and work hard, and it is his teachings I have carried forward into my own coaching and speaking business, the clients I now work with benefit from the expertise of a great leader. I can't thank Billal enough for what he brought out in me.

My biggest thanks will always go to my family. I would not have achieved all that I have without the continued support of my husband Barry and my three sons Christopher, Leighton and Joseph. Their support and encouragement are what drive me forward every day.

About the Author

Angela Preston, also the author of Opening Doors, is known for her zest and passion for empowering individuals through her workshops and talks. She is a recognized influence on confidence and personal development. She is a regular guest on both radio and TV and recently shared her expertise in a TV interview and book launch with C-Suite Network as part of Best Seller TV in New York. Angela also delivers impact workshops based on the content of this book. With her authentic and welcoming personality, Angela leaves the clients believing there is no limit to what can be achieved.

She trained with the Public Speaking Academy and the Coaching Academy when embarking on her new career as a speaker/coach.

Angela has twenty years experience in sales and leadership as a top-performing strategic manager prior to becoming a speaker/author.

Angela believes we all have it within us to achieve the ultimate and become great at being us. She inspires her clients to make the impossible become the possible and never give up on their dreams.

For more information and contact details about Angela and her work, please visit www.angelaprestoncoaching.com.

Contents

Introduction

When I sat down and started writing my first book, *Opening Doors*, I honestly didn't have a clue what I was doing. But what I did know was how important it was to get my message out to as many people as possible. I wanted to inspire them to be the best versions of themselves they could possibly be. No matter what situation you find yourself in or the background from which you came, there is always light at the end of the tunnel. You just have to keep searching and never give up.

During all of the adversity I found myself in over the years, there were numerous times I felt like giving up and throwing in the towel. Yet always in the back of my mind, I believed I had a lot to offer and knew that others could benefit from my experiences and learn from how I overcame the many trials and tribulations I faced.

I didn't know how to put a book together. I had my memories and just had to work out how to put them down on paper so others would not only want to read my book but also want to talk about how it changed their lives. That was the reason for writing the book in the beginning. After writing the first few pages, I realised it could help others. If I could influence one person to change his or her life after reading my book, I had done a whole lot more than become an author. I believe that whatever we get out of this life, we should put back to help others.

The tenth of July 2014 is vivid in my memory, when I first sat down to learn how to write a book. After researching motivational speakers, I came across Brendon Burchard. His advice was to write a book to build up your credibility. Now here I was, following his advice. If I was to follow my dreams and become someone who inspires others, I had to listen to those who had been there before me.

I looked at a number of websites before coming across one about Joseph Campbell. If ever I questioned my path and whether I was on the right one, this now confirmed it. Writing my book was the right decision for me.

My first book was written in memory of my parents, especially my mum, and the wonderful foundation of love she built for each of her six girls to grow. Yes, we may have had very little in terms of material goods, but the family values, and morals she instilled in each of us set us up for life. No matter what life throws our way, we can overcome it.

and his name cemented that writing was to become my new vocation. I had a message others needed to hear, and my mum gave me her approval to follow my heart.

They say things don't happen by accident. The people we meet come into our lives for a reason, so I believe my mum directed me to this website to let me know this was my path and to continue on it. My mum's maiden name was Josephine Campbell. If this wasn't a message, I don't know what was. This was no coincidence; this really was a message from the woman who made me the person I am today.

I described in my book the bond she had, not just with myself and my sisters, but also with her grandchildren and the people she met throughout her life. Thirteen years after her death, people I meet still speak of the impact she had on them. This kind of gift to empower and inspire others is inside each of us; we just have to look deep enough for it.

As well as wanting to help others believe in themselves and show them how to overcome adversity, I also want to create a tool with which parents and children can build unbreakable bonds that will enhance their growth. When children are supported and encouraged to follow their dreams, this creates a belief within them that they can achieve what they set their hearts on. It also gives them the confidence to go out and achieve it, even in families that live on the breadline and have the bare minimum of food. I am living proof that if you set goals from childhood, doing so becomes second nature, and when you are an adult, your expectations and aspirations just keep growing.

We all base success on different factors. For me, success means inspiring my children as well as others to go out and live their best lives and achieve their dreams. I could only do this by finding my own purpose in life and making it my mission to achieve it. Along the way, we may get sidetracked and taken off course for a little while. But by taking one step at a time, we move closer to reaching our goals. Others may say luck plays a part in success, but you first have to have action within you to find that luck. I believe everyone has action within them, but self-doubts and limiting beliefs stops many of us in our tracks.

We often question how certain individuals – like Richard Branson, Tony Robbins, and Oprah Winfrey – have it all, but what we forget is what they have done to achieve success. The key is they were willing to take risks, work hard, and step out of their comfort zones. This is necessary if you are to achieve your dreams. They didn't wait for opportunity to find them; they went out and searched for it. That is why they are successful in their chosen careers.

As a child, I looked at stars on TV or in papers and magazines and wondered what types of backgrounds they came from to be who they were. Being so young, I thought only people from privileged backgrounds could become successful. It was only as I got older that I realised some of these stars had upbringings similar to mine. They just didn't give up. They chased their dreams. We often associate success with money, power, and material things, but the biggest success comes from deep within. Fulfilling our inner desire for success brings us the life we truly desire.

I am here to tell you that no matter what your upbringing or what you are struggling with, you have success within you. Even if you fail over and over, the key is to never give up. Thomas Edison claimed to have failed ten thousand times before coming up with the light bulb. So since childhood, I have never given up. Why? From failure comes success; we just learn what not to do the next time.

If you are going to achieve success, you need to be bold and brave to stand out. You can't let the opinions of others drown out your own voice.

On 8 May 2014, I resigned from my well-paid corporate job; that decision was probably the boldest and bravest I would ever make. It took a lot of courage and soul-searching before I decided to quit. I could have easily carried on doing the job I was programmed to do, working up to fifteen-hour days, but my yearning to lead a fulfilled existence and follow the path I was put on this earth for far outweighed my fear. I wanted to become the person God created me to be. I wanted to fulfil my desire to help others find their purpose and lead lives that make their hearts sing when they wake up, as well as make their hearts jump with joy. That desire made the decision to quit easier.

Since beginning my journey to become an author, coach, and motivational speaker, I have grown to a level I never thought possible. I have shared the stage with TV stars and worked with some amazing people. I have been on radio stations and been featured in the media. Yes, this has been incredible, but the biggest accolade for me has been raising funds for wonderful charities. Before resigning from my job, I had always donated money but did not have the time to give. Now I donate a whole day each week to help raise funds as well as putting events together. I am truly living the life I missed out on for so long. If we give just a little of our time to a worthy cause, we can make such a difference in people's lives, which is worth anything we could ever wish to achieve in our careers.

I believe we learn from doing and not dreaming. Do something every day that takes you closer to your goal. Life is for living, and when you find your purpose in life, that is when you truly start living. Richard Branson once said, "The best advice I could give anyone is spend your time working on what you are passionate about in life." This is so true.

Your passion is linked to your purpose. It is the one thing that wakes you up through the night because you are too excited to sleep, thinking about what the day ahead will bring as well as how you can benefit others.

That is why I decided to resign. I had always thought my passion was in the job I was doing, but that was masked by the results I was getting. I had taken a year off for health reasons, and while away from work, I realised that my passion was helping people become the very best versions of themselves.

I thought improving the locations I was going into was making my heart skip a beat, when in actual fact it was the journey I was going on with the people I was working with that gave me the greatest feeling inside. Watching them grow on a daily basis and become great at what they were doing was worth every mile I travelled. My greatest pleasure was to help guide them in their quest for success.

Now I knew what it was I really wanted to do. Did I have it within me to succeed and, more importantly, to reach even higher than I had done? Even though I was successful in my role at my company, that feeling of fulfilment was not there. I also felt a yearning inside to grow as an individual and to give more. If I continued in this job, I may have been limiting myself. I would say to anyone thinking of making a change, whether it is in their personal or business life, go for it; you will never know what you can achieve unless you take a risk and step outside your comfort zone.

As I stated earlier, the stars I watched on television and read about all those years ago took a chance and it paid off; not all risks will pay off, but they are the best lessons for us to learn from. If you keep knocking, doors will eventually open. Mine did.

After I resigned, I had three months in which to decide if it really was what I wanted. The first night after handing in my resignation, I slept for fourteen hours. I knew it was the right decision. I had not slept for more than four hours per night in the previous two years; not because my heart skipped a beat when I thought of the day ahead, nor the excitement of what the day would bring, more how I dreaded going into the job. Two years before, even though I would be travelling on the motorway eight times a day to get to and from work, my heart did skip a beat because I was excited to be doing a job I loved. Eventually, however, I wasn't sleeping for very different reasons.

I still didn't know what I would do or how I would do it, but just like when we are babies and don't know how to crawl or walk, we don't give up at the first fall. We keep going until we master it, and this was no different. I would soon learn how to write a book and how to become a motivational speaker, and I would make sure I would be just as good (if not better) at this as I was as an area manager or any of the previous roles I had.

Within a month of resigning, my passion for getting results was no longer there. I stopped getting excited at the thought; this really did confirm for me what I already knew. The saying "If you enjoy your job, you will never work a day in your life" had always played a part in my career; from the first day of being a self-employed agent through to September 2012, I had danced my way through every day with a spring in my step, knowing I was doing a job I loved. Now that I was no longer getting that feeling. It was time to find it again; the only way I was going to feel like this again was to do what I wanted and follow my heart.

As a motivational coach/speaker, I had to prove I was capable of coaching others through not just their darkest times, but also changes they wanted to make, whether that be their personal lives or business lives. First, I had to demonstrate to them how I had been in their very position and what I had done to come out of it, stronger and wiser. I had to shift my mind-set on how I would make a successful career change from an area manager to an author whose experiences would benefit others.

All that I had learned as a child would serve me to make that change and make a success of it; even if I didn't have the answers right now, I would figure them out along the way, just as I had previously done.

I once listened to an interview with Jack Canfield, who said, "When you have a goal, don't think of how you will achieve it, just write it down, as the answer comes along later." I learned this to be true and follow this pattern whenever I want to achieve a new goal; as long as we know what our goal is, the how will work itself out as we work towards accomplishing it.

I have always believed we should only regret the things we haven't done, not the things we have; the actor/comedian Jim Carrey said, "You can fail doing what you don't want, so you might as well take a chance on doing what you love." Even though I was taking a risk, I knew it would pay off, and if I have inspired one person to do the same, then I have achieved what I set out to do.

My desire is to help others become the person they have always been inside and lead the life they were born to live; nothing could stand in my way to becoming that person.

Now that I had resigned and had an idea about what I wanted to do and the person I wished to become, how was I going to do that?

First, I had to start by drawing on previous experiences and how I had overcome them and what actions I took. I had to first of all change or adjust my mind-set; yes, I had been successful when I was self-employed and when I was an area manager, but this was on a completely different level.

We all have that little voice in our heads telling us we can't achieve our dreams or we are not even worthy enough to achieve them, but that voice was not going to stop me. I kept telling myself, "Who am I not to achieve it? I am worthy of becoming a published author." Daily positive affirmations are something I live by. If I was to make others change their whole lives and believe in themselves, I had to first show them how it was done. I believe behind every door is a new and fresh opportunity for us all to start a new beginning. That is why my first book was titled *Opening Doors*; whether what is behind them is for us, only we can make that decision, and no matter what door I went through, whether when I was child of sixteen and walking into a fancy store with my first week's salary to buy some new clothes, and knowing when I walked out anything was possible if I set my mind on it, to achieving my biggest dream of running a branch office and then deciding to walk away from that job because it was no longer fulfilling.

The one thing I could always count on has been the belief I have in myself; when you have this, there is no limits to what can be done. The world truly is your oyster, and this is what I have continually taught my three boys. Whatever else I taught them in life, my biggest lesson was always the belief they can be, do, and have whatever they want in their lives. I would tell anyone who is struggling right now, work on your mind-set. Change your thoughts from "I can't, I don't know how" to "I can, I will, and I did," and your whole life will change before your very eyes. Every door you walk through thereafter will be a lesson you will take away, whether it is something you won't do again or something you could have done differently or even something you will definitely do again.

Behind every door is a new and great opportunity, if you want it to be. My own self-belief took me from being a self-employed agent (I did not really understand that role) to earning a full-time salary for part-time hours, to now writing my second book. Even though I didn't originally know where to start, my self-belief kept pushing me forward over the years to continue to reach for more.

Of course, you can't get by just on self-belief; you also have to have action. No matter how much you believe in your own abilities, without action, you will stand still. Put the two together, and you can become anything you choose to be. I want you to realise that achieving the ultimate is not as hard as you may think.

When I wrote *Opening Doors* and was talking with friends, some of them reminded me of how I had always spoken about writing a book; when I was younger, I had the desire to become a journalist, so it actually made sense to go down the route of becoming a writer, but first I had to go through the experiences I have to fulfil that desire. Things come to us when we are ready for them; no matter how strong that desire inside, we have to be ready to take on the challenge, and we also must ensure we don't miss it.

Throughout our lives, we will get messages that we may not always understand until we are supposed to, but who are we to question them? My purpose was not revealed to me until I was in my late forties. Age is just a number; never think you are too old to find the path you are meant to be on. Colonel Sanders was sixty-five when he founded Kentucky Fried Chicken, proving it is never too late.

In this book I will discuss the ten keys I used to achieve success. I am not saying these keys will take you to your ultimate desire, because everyone has different goals or different dreams, but it will give you an idea of what you can do to help yourself take that extra step towards your heart's desire.

KEY 1

Vision

The first thing we have to do is find what doors we want to open. The first key I used in my quest to become an author, coach, and speaker is the one I believe to be the most important one, as without this, we won't get very far.

A few years ago, when I decided I wanted to do something different, I wasn't sure what I was lacking. I soon realised the vital key I needed to ensure the success I wanted was vision. By not having a vision, I was stopping myself moving forward.

When we have a goal and clarify what that goal is, our vision is formed; when we bake a cake, we must have the right ingredients to begin with. First and foremost, we have to have the main ingredient to ensure the cake tastes right, and that is the same when you want to accomplish something.

As time went on and my vision became clearer, I started to believe I would reach my goal. I also suggest you link it with your passion; once you do this, the chances of you failing become minimal. You see, passion is what will push you forward when you feel like giving up.

I am the most impatient person and want things done yesterday, but I am also realistic and know that it doesn't happen that way, so my vision is what keeps me focused. When you are setting a goal, you have to begin with the end in mind; this is also clarifying your vision, and then you break it down into small chunks. Many people fail at their first attempt and maybe even their second, but the one thing that makes successful people carry on is the vision they can see in front of them. This is what keeps them believing and moving forward; these successful individuals are living proof how important this key is. Without it, you are never getting off the starting line.

Stephen Spielberg was rejected from film school three times before actually being accepted; imagine what the world would have missed out on if he did not have a vision that kept him focused on the end result.

Oprah Winfrey, another example of a visionary person, was fired as a TV reporter because they didn't think she had what it took. Oprah had a strong vision and achieved her goal. She became not just an iconic presenter adored by millions but a beacon of light to women across the world who also have a dream they want to fulfil. Her story makes them believe the impossible can become possible. Her company, Harpo, is one of the richest companies in the world; if she had lacked vision, how many people would have missed out?

Martin Luther King Jr. made one of the most famous speeches of our time. His dream and vision was for all in the United States to be equal; it is among the most acclaimed speeches in US history. If he did not have this vision of a fairer society in which every person is equal, how many lives would have been affected?

Thomas Edison proved that you can succeed even if you fail at something one, two, or even three times. There is a chance you may say to yourself, "This is not for me," but Edison didn't fail just a few times. It is hard to believe that someone can fail the number of times he did and still keep going.

How did he carry on after so many failed attempts? What was going through his mind each time he failed? Whatever it was, it was never going to stop him; his vision was so strong that he knew in his heart he would get it right one day, and he eventually invented the long-lasting practical electric light bulb as well as the phonograph and the motion picture camera.

These four people show the difference between having a vision and not having one. Ordinary individuals around the world would not have achieved success in their chosen paths had they not had a strong vision. What is a vision, and how do we know what it looks like?

It is a picture in our mind of what we want to happen; once we envision this, we are telling our subconscious what we want, and this will make it happen for us, just like Jack Canfield's statement about writing goals down. It is also that feeling in your stomach that tells you to keep going. It is the one thing that will keep you awake at night looking for solutions as to how you will accomplish it, as well as the feeling inside. It will also provide you with an insight into how your future will look.

CEOs have a vision of where they want their company to go and how to ensure revenue is increased. This is important if they are to avoid obstacles or at least be ready for them when they do occur, because sure enough, they will. They need to plan accordingly when change is needed.

It will also keep them motivated and inspired to keep growing. Keeping their vision at the forefront of their mind stops them from giving up.

As the leader of the company, all the employees will look to them for guidance, so it is paramount their vision is crystal-clear to ensure communication is managed in the right way. With a vision, obstacles and challenges will seem irrelevant, ensuring that every setback or mistake results in a lesson learned.

Having a vision also provides focus, which can sometimes be missing. This is another key ingredient to the success of any business. Being focused helps you avoid day-to-day distractions that may otherwise stop you moving forward towards your goals. You can develop a strategy around your vision, once you are clear what it is.

Knowing what my vision was pushed me on, even in the early days before resigning from my job. This kept my mind focused on what I needed to do and how I would achieve it.

When I first researched great leaders, change makers, and influential people, I didn't really know who I was looking for or how I was going to become this person. I envisioned myself on a stage, sharing my story with the world; no matter where in life you start off, you don't have to stay there. Only you can change your destiny, but you can get guidance and support, and you can also emulate others. Ultimately, only you can make the changes happen.

Once you have this vision, nothing can stand in your way. You will do everything in your power to get there. I am exactly like the next person. During this wonderful journey I am on, I made certain decisions that didn't help me, and quite a number of times, I felt like giving up, but that vision drove me until I achieved my goal, whether it is to open a school in India for street kids or a homeless shelter in Liverpool that will cater for every single one of their needs. I hope my first key has given you an insight as to where you start when embarking on a new venture or even just to make a change you haven't yet made. Just make sure your vision is crystal-clear.

KEY 2

Self-Belief

This now links on to my second key. Yes, vision is the main key, and without it, your goal will not be achieved, so keeping your vision strong is vital when it comes to achieving, but visualising isn't enough if you lack my second key: self-belief.

I have used self-belief right throughout my life; I start with this when I begin working with a new client. If I am coaching clients or delivering a workshop, self-belief will be high on the agenda on how to keep progressing and moving forward.

When we set out to accomplish a goal, we must believe inside we are going to achieve it. If we don't, that dream will stay just a dream. I have used self-belief my whole life through, from a little girl living in Radcliffe Walk with the bare minimum of food and getting lost in the world of *Black Beauty* on TV through to today, as a published author. This is what I draw on when I am struggling to see the forest for the trees.

I then think back to my mum's words of how we could be anything we choose to be if we are willing to search within. Even if you think you have gone far enough, keep searching, as sometimes, you have go to a place you've never been before to uncover it. The belief she had in each of us is what taught me to always have the self-belief to imagine that whatever you want, it is there for you, if you are willing to grow and learn the skills along the way that will support you in your new venture. This second key is one of the most important keys I used to open the doors to success.

As a leader, it is great to have a vision so you know where you are going, although you must have the belief in yourself that you will get there. If you want an extraordinary life, you must believe you are worthy of it. I have learned over the years how important it is to have self-belief.

When we made an offer on our first home, my husband was ready to walk out, because he felt that we couldn't afford it; he also didn't want me to build my hopes up in case we failed, but I knew inside that the house would be ours. Why? No matter what it took, the belief I was carrying to realise my dream of owning our home pushed me forward to own it. As another example, when I resigned and walked away from the comfort of a monthly paycheque, friends thought I was going a little crazy and having a midlife crisis. I didn't get into a debate with them, because I knew once I make a decision, nothing will keep me from achieving it.

Self-belief plays a huge part in your success; it determines if you take that leap of faith or stay within the confines of your comfort zone. Even though I was annoyed at people's comments, I also understand that not everyone believes in their own abilities, so why would they believe in someone else's? When you don't have self-belief, it can affect how you live your life; you accept things that someone with self-belief wouldn't.

A belief is something we tell ourselves; that can be a positive or a negative affirmation. When we hear that voice in our heads, if it is negative, we must banish it immediately and change it to a positive one, as this is how we build self-belief. The more we tell ourselves we can do something, the more we are coaching our minds to believe anything is within reach. The only person who has the right to live rent-free in your mind is you. Only you can decide whether you have self-belief or not; no one else has the right to make that decision without you agreeing to it. So when you hear friends, family, colleagues, or coworkers tell you it can't be done, you show them what can be accomplished with self-belief; remember, it is their belief about themselves, not yours.

Remember, self-belief can be formed at any point in our lives; mine was formed from a very young age, but not everyone's is.

A manager I worked under for a very short time told me she thought I was overconfident; she thought by using these words, I would somehow form a picture in my mind of what I was supposed to be like, which would then stop me from achieving the results I was achieving on a regular basis and become a follower instead of paving my own path. She thought by putting me down, it would affect how I saw myself going forward, when in reality, I posed a threat to her. I got results and managed others with respect and integrity. She somehow felt threatened by how I was able to build teams, but as always, her words were like water off a duck's back to me. She didn't know I wasn't interested in her job; I could have done her job with my eyes closed, but I chose not to. It wasn't challenging enough and was not part of my future plan, and that is why I chose to walk away and follow my own path.

When I looked around the company where I worked, the majority of leaders were now of the same mentality: if you beat someone down enough and keep telling them they are a certain type, they start to believe it. That is when you become a robot, so when someone says that you are overconfident, remember it is their opinion of themselves. Great leaders support and encourage their teams to grow.

Not everyone has self-belief from a young age; for some, it comes after acquiring more experience or skills. For others like myself, it is instilled by your parents. My three sons have tons of self-belief and are always willing to come out of their comfort zone and do the things others are afraid to do. They all worked in America in summer camps from eighteen; without self-belief, they would not have been able to do it year after year.

When we first come into this world, we are not conditioned to be good or bad at anything; we decide this as we encounter new things that happen. We limit ourselves on what we can and can't do, and this is when we start forming our self-belief, but we don't have to always have little or no self-belief. It is something we can work on. One way of re-evaluating your own limiting beliefs about yourself is to examine what your idea of self-belief stands for. There are numerous book on limiting beliefs and how to improve them or how to get rid of them completely. When you question yourself, is it your voice or the voice of others ringing in your ears? Usually, it is the voice of others, maybe an old school teacher, a parent, a partner, or even a friend. Colleagues who don't want to move out of their own comfort zone may be unhappy for you to do the same. It could be their voice that is helping you form your own beliefs about yourself.

When I was in junior school, I had very little concentration and sat outside the head teacher's office more than I was at my desk. I quite regularly heard, "Angela Riley, you will never amount to anything." Looking back, I could so easily have believed this teacher and limited myself to what I could achieve, but I chose not to, and even though I did have low concentration levels, I always had the belief my situation would improve.

These voices can sometimes come disguised as our own, and that is when we limit ourselves, which keeps us from becoming the best we can be. Repeat to yourself, "This is not my voice." We become what we think; if you think you can't, you won't, and if you think you can, you will. Our thoughts hold the keys to our future, so if you believe you can conquer the world, then that is what will happen.

There is a quote I carry every day, which I believe is the difference between achieving success and not achieving it: "Almost every successful person begins with two beliefs: the future can be better than the present, and I have the power to make it so." If you say this to yourself every day, your life will change beyond measure.

KEY 3

Confidence

Once you know where you are heading and you believe in your own ability to get there, you then have to make sure you follow through, or the first two keys will not work for you. No matter how strong your vision is or how much you believe in your goal, you must be prepared to execute it. My third key is a very important cog on your wheel to success. That key is confidence. Confidence goes hand-in-hand with self-belief, as without either of these keys, I would not be writing my second book. It can also be built at any time throughout our lives. It is psychological, and with a structure in place of how to build it, the changes you are looking for can be found at a time when you are ready to learn it.

When you are confident, you can take on any task put in front of you. This also builds self-belief, so if you are low on self-belief, a quick way to improve it is to work on your confidence.

Confident people will also display an air of positivity about themselves. They believe this shows when you are confident in what you are doing, you also tell others they can have confidence in you; you can speak honestly and not worry about what others think.

Self-confident people face fears head-on and take risks; they know whatever obstacles that are placed in their way they have the ability to overcome them. Although confidence can be learned, it is very much a state of mind. With positive thinking, training, practice, and knowledge of your chosen subject, your confidence will soar. Building on your knowledge of things improves your competence, which in turn improves your confidence.

Confident people always produce high results, especially leaders, as they are role models for others to aspire to be. This confidence comes from years of experience and self-acceptance, whether that be mind or body, and the belief in your own ability and that is why only certain individuals make great leaders, as not everyone has the ability to be confident in both areas.

Having low confidence doesn't have to last forever; it is like any skill. It can be taught and learnt at any time, as long as you practice and build on skills or knowledge you have already acquired.

Although I have always believed in my abilities, there have been plenty of times when my confidence has been knocked, which can affect how you work and behave, as well as how others see you. Everyone wants to be around confident people and learn from them; it is completely different with people who lack confidence. Some people will put them down, affecting their confidence even more, and others will have no faith in them. They may be bypassed for a promotion or a new role; even though you may have self-belief, it doesn't mean you have confidence, which could affect your whole future.

I can talk about a number of times when my confidence was knocked so bad I really didn't think I could come back, but the biggest one and probably the hardest one was before I resigned from my job. That was the lowest point in my life; how was I going to come back from the knocks I had continually took in the previous two years? This was something that went over and over in my mind. To build my confidence back up, I had to draw on previous successes and tell myself I hadn't come this far to then stop. For two years, I had been under the doctor, as well as having to have cognitive behavioural therapy to help me overcome the events of the previous two years. I was starting to question my own ability, even though I had been successful for so long, but what I wasn't taking into account at the time: it was the actions of others that was affecting my confidence and not from anything I was doing.

My confidence had taken a battering, and at that point in time, I was unsure if I would recover. This lasted for a number of weeks after I resigned. Even though my decision to leave was the right one, I was even questioning that; my confidence was that low. I wasn't even capable of making a decision, and that was why I was questioning whether I had made the right choice. Some questions kept going through my head: should I have just carried on and maybe things would have changed? Would I ever have the success I had previously had? But the one question that went over and over in my mind, day after day, was, will I ever be happy again and smile from my soul, as I had always done up until the previous two years, and then I was told by the doctor, of course it is normal to have all these feelings of emotion and questions I needed answering.

Change is something that is hard for all of us, and when it comes when you are not really ready for it, then it is that bit harder. I had been thinking of resigning for a while, but it was still the most difficult decision to make, as I didn't know what effect it would have on not just me but also my family. My salary had provided so much for us over the years, and to now be walking away from that with nothing in place took a lot of courage, but that shows how low I really was. When you know in your heart you are taking a huge gamble, but you have no other choice, then the decision that comes is the right one, and as hard as it was, I knew what my decision had to be.

After I left my job, I thought of all the previous trials and tribulations, the death of my parents, the accident that would disable my husband for life, and a near-death experience I myself had faced, and realised this was actually a walk in the park for me. If I was still here after all this, then leaving a job would not destroy me nor my confidence any more than it already had. I decided there and then I would not be defeated;

my self-belief is what has pushed me forward to build my confidence up in the past, and that is what would happen again.

You should also be aware that others may view your confidence as arrogance or even self-obsession. I may have been guilty of it in the past; when we are successful, we may not even realise we have become this person. A little bit of self-awareness can bring us back down to the humble person we have always been.

There will also be times on your journey you may have to change your circle of friends; not everyone understands where you are right now and why you are looking for change. They may question your actions, or it may be a simple negative comment, again just like if we become overconfident, they may not even realise they are doing it, but this kind of behaviour can have a huge impact on you, and you then start to question yourself on why you should have the success you want, which will have an impact on your confidence.

I am not saying remove these people from your life; just don't spend a lot of time with them. This helps you make strides towards building your confidence. They say you become the average of the five people you spend the most time with; ensure you surround yourself with people who are on the same as yourself and those who are supportive of your journey.

I myself have had to walk away from individuals who I previously had considered friends. It is not a bad thing; it just means we are all on our own individual journey, and not everyone will understand yours.

Being positive even in negative situations stops you focusing on what is in the way and shows how you will overcome it. It is so important to divert your energy and focus towards solutions rather than problems. When interacting with others, always portray a positive outlook; for example, smile more and use eye contact when talking to people. Just standing tall with your shoulders in place gives the impression you are a confident person. They say smiles are the best medicine; it brightens not only your day but also others you may greet. When you envision a self-confident person, they are someone with posture and a smile. Be that person.

KEY 4

Optimism

The fourth key I have carried right throughout my life, and will continue to do so, is as important to me as my vision. When I first set out on this journey of self-discovery, if I did not have this, then my idea of the perfect life and being abundantly happy in all areas of my life would not have happened. For me, this is the one key that could have stopped me in my tracks when I was having a difficult day and looking for answers to the questions that were continually going over in my mind, and that key is optimism.

Optimism represents staying positive in difficult or adverse situations and believing that things will improve; with optimism, you lead the life you choose to lead. Thinking positively can also boost your physical and mental state; seeing a glass as half-full rather than half-empty is the first step to being optimistic. Whenever I have faced difficult situations in my life, whether that be my personal or business life, I have always kept an optimistic view that things can only get better. By keeping this mind-set, I ensure whatever was happening in the present moment, it would not continue, and I would one day understand why I had to go through those times to get to the next destination on my journey of life.

Having an optimistic outlook has served me well from childhood; with a positive mind, I was always on my way to a better and brighter future, one that would not just benefit me with material goods, but also provide that inner feeling of fulfilment when encouraging and inspiring others to follow their hearts and achieve their dreams.

It is sometimes very difficult to stay positive in difficult or adverse situations, but by doing so, you are sending out signals your future will be better than your present, no matter how things might be at that moment.

Just like negativity breeds negativity, so does positivity, and when we are around optimistic people, we suddenly become positive about our own future; optimistic people seem to give off an aroma. Pessimism and optimism are infectious, so my advice is to always surround yourself with optimistic people, who are always looking at a half-full glass. They say we become the average of the five people we spend the most time with; by ensuring you spend time with people who are on the same journey as yourself, you are more likely to succeed.

Pessimistic people and their thoughts will be, why haven't I got what others have got, why can't things be different for me, or why do things go wrong for me, they will always have a half-empty glass when looking at a difficult situation. People who are very pessimistic will always have a way of looking at things in a dark way and with a closed mind, they are the ones who will always look for the negative in everything. when you have an open mind it is paving the way for new opportunities to come your way. When we are optimistic we look for opportunities in every problem we may face.

Here's an example of being optimistic in a difficult situation. Not long after I got my first role as a development manager, an agent who had over three hundred customers decided to leave. I was left to sort out the agency before I could even contemplate recruiting for it. I didn't have much experience at the time, as I had only been in my role for a couple of months, and remember thinking, *How can I turn this around?*

The week after the position became vacant, I was attending a course at the head office and got talking to a senior manager. I started telling him about my vacancy and asking his advice on what he would do in my position; never be afraid to ask others for help who have been there before, as you will be surprised how much easier and quicker it is to work something out rather than trying to come up with the answers yourself. Also, always accept constructive criticism, as someone else's opinion can be worth quite a lot if it saves you making the same mistake twice. I carried his advice right throughout my career and also relayed it to others who were faced with the same situation.

I can still hear his voice telling me to look at the opportunity the agent leaving had presented to me rather than the problems. They say always find a solution before you encounter a problem. The advice this man was giving me was invaluable at the time; having an optimistic outlook anyway made my mind open up to all possibilities. I took on board what he was saying and realised the growth potential I had right in front of me to build not just a bigger section with higher revenue, but also a stronger one. Through this man leaving, I would be able to split the agency, giving me the option to recruit two new agents. By doing this, I would generate more revenue, and by me training these agents, they would be working to the standards I would create rather than what someone before me had created. His advice had me all excited at going back to the branch to get things in motion; before I had left for the course, I was actually dreading the thought of going back, as I knew what I was going back to. The thought of this huge agency and the issues I would be presented with had me worried about going back, but after this one conversation, my whole mind-set had changed. I realised that if we face every challenge with optimism, then anything is possible.

On my return to the branch, I did split the agency, as this was the right thing to do. I worked every hour to turn it into two quality agencies with high earning commissions to be made, ensuring I could recruit two agents who would continue the hard work it had taken to turn it around. The job of a development manager wasn't for the fainthearted or the lazy; you had to work hard to get results, and I had worked myself to the bone to make sure I would benefit in the long run.

Those two agencies not only built revenue, they also built a strong team, one which would go on to be top of the branch and win numerous awards for hard work, not just from myself but also my agents. One of the agents I recruited actually influenced my decision years later to emigrate to Spain, so had it not been for that one conversation with a stranger on how to overcome challenges, I would not have looked at it with the optimism I did and I may not have gotten the results I did. I certainly would not have had the experience of living in another country and sampling a different culture.

This is one of the reasons I have included optimism as a key to success. There will always be times in our lives we will find it hard to be optimistic; we may have to dig deep and go to a place we haven't been before to find it. I say to anyone, no matter what you face, keeping that optimistic outlook will bring you out the other side stronger and wiser.

KEY 5

Determination

Key 5 played a major role in getting me where I am today; in my first book, I wrote about how my dad instilled the importance of determination in each of his six girls.

With this key, everything you have wanted in your life is there for the taking. I have always had this in abundance; I used to watch this trait show itself in all its glory when my dad would be doing something or talking of issues he was dealing with. As a very young child, I always observed the behaviour of others and learned from them; by watching my dad, I learned that whatever you go after in life, determination plays a key role in whether you will achieve it.

This key has helped define the person I have become and is also one of my strongest traits. I feel I will be successful at whatever I pursue in life; it may take a long time, but having determination means I will never fail, no matter how long it takes. Without this key, you may not achieve what you are pursuing; no matter how much you want circumstances to improve, you can only make these changes yourself. It is determination that will decide if you fail or succeed; when you have determination, a positive mind, and an optimistic outlook, you can keep pushing through, and the answers will show themselves along the way.

The determination to keep going was embedded in me as a little girl; from the age of five, I would write down my goals. As young as I was,

I knew only I was responsible for what sort of life I had; when I got older and gave birth to my children, I knew if I was to give them the start in life I didn't have, then I had to have the determination to keep progressing forward.

So what does determination mean to me as an individual? it means I am building a skill from within that would serve me throughout my life, ensuring whatever I set my mind on I can make it happen. I also see it as being happy in all areas of my life. Yes, we all want to live a stress-free life without money worries, but abundance for me was also that feeling inside that when I leave this world, I have made a positive difference in some small way.

One quote I live by was written by Brendan Burchard: "At the end of our lives, we all ask, 'Did I live? Did I love? Did I matter?'"

For me, this quote reflects the person I am; the greatest gift you can give someone is your time and your teachings. If you help others to improve their lives, this quote will resonate with you as it does with me.

When I got older, I realised the meaning of the word "determination" and how lucky I am to have this skill. Not everyone is lucky enough to have it.

There are times when we all feel like giving up and walking away, me included. I mentioned earlier in the book a couple of times when I really found it hard to keep going; each time I felt like throwing in the towel, my dad's voice would ring in my ears: "Where is your determination? I didn't raise you to give up," and that voice would soon jolt me back to reality. The reasons I am doing what I am doing would come flooding back, and that all-important value, which I thought was gone, would show itself again.

Throughout our lives, determination will show when we need it most. I am no different from the next person; what will define us is how we use it. The hardest thing I ever had to overcome was the death of my mum. I never imagined life without her, as it was just too painful to even contemplate, and even when we were informed she only had three months left to live, I was still in denial and carried on as normal.

When I look back, it was wishful thinking that it would all go away; there would be a miracle and somehow my mum would recover. When she did pass over, I thought my life was going to end right there. Even though I was a mum myself, I felt like I had lost my ability to be both a mum and a woman; I wondered how I would come out of this intact. It was only after an accident three weeks later that could so easily have taken my husband did I realise how lucky I really was. This accident was catastrophic, and he could no longer do what he had previously done, but he was alive, and that is all that mattered. The day after he was admitted to hospital, I woke up with a very different mind-set from the one I had gone to bed with.

Sometimes, when trials appear in our lives and tragedies happen, we may feel powerless to deal with them; we may even consider ourselves as victims, asking ourselves, "Why me?" I did just that; in the beginning, I felt we were victims and that question was going round in my head.

That day, I woke up and realised I was no more a victim than the person down the street who had lost her parents or someone whose husband walked out. It was life, and these things happen; how we will deal with it determines whether we let life define us or we define life, and that is when the determination within came to the surface when I needed it most. So I decided there and then I would think of my mum with love and joy, rather than tears and sadness. I would recall all the happy memories we had made over thirty-five years rather than the previous three months, and I would stand up and take the reins, just as my mum expected me to.

I knew our lives had changed dramatically, not just from the loss of my mum and my husband's accident, but also from the financial implications of the loss of my husband's salary. It was then I thought back to the promises I had made to myself when I was a little girl: no matter what we faced as a family, my children would never feel the impact of it; their lives would not change in any way. They had to face the prospect of losing their nan and an accident that could very easily have taken their dad, and that was enough for them to deal with as far as I was concerned. These facts were out of my control. I could not let my children avoid them, but what I could do was make sure the loss of my husband's salary would not affect them any more than they had already been affected.

With sheer determination and tenacity, I worked extra hours, ensuring what we lost I made up for with bonuses.

Determination has always kept me focused and pushed me to never give up; I have a competitiveness to keep striving for more. I was still feeling the loss of my mum and my husband's accident, but I had a new focus, which was stronger than any obstacle I faced, and that was to give my boys the future they deserved.

Determination continued to grow inside me as the years went on. After I had written my first book and had used up all my savings to get it published, I realised there were no funds left to actually market the book. I knew this was the hard part; the writing and publishing was the easy part. If I was to promote the book, I had to come up with a plan, but with very limited funds, how was I going to do that?

I knew for the book to have the best chance of success, I had to reach a wide audience, and the only way to do that was to put a strategy together. With determination to make it work, I set about compiling a strategy; there was definitely no option but to make it work. Sometimes, when we are backed into a corner, that is when everything we have inside shows itself. I was not prepared to write fifty-two thousand words for it to just sit on a shelf; that would not benefit the people I wanted to reach.

After the book was published, I set a budget to launch the book and start my promotional campaign; for it to be a success, I had to target the right audience. I started by putting together an email template that I could send out to the media as well as libraries and bookstores. My launch was 14 August, and I had to get word of mouth out before the date to ensure it was a success. I started with local radio stations and was completely shocked to get a reply from Pete Price's producer at Radio City, inviting me onto his show as a guest on 12 August. That interview proved very successful, as listeners who heard the programme actually attended the launch two days later. That was my very first interview; I was excited but also terrified of how I would come across on the radio; would I come across likeable and authentic? We all like to be liked, and being authentic is the biggest value I carry through life.

With no previous experience of this kind, I was taking a chance; it could have gone either way. The day of the interview, my nerves were getting the better of me; I didn't know the first thing about being interviewed on the radio. I didn't know what questions would be asked, so I could not prepare. I was treading on unfamiliar territory; I am usually so organised and prepared for everything, so this was affecting me in a big way. I wanted the listeners to come away from that interview feeling inspired enough to go out and follow their dreams, and this is where my determination kicked in when I needed it. Although I didn't know what would be asked, I was determined to leave a positive effect with both Pete and his listeners, and that is what it did.

I then decided to turn the launch into a fundraising night for a local youth club and set about on a mission to gather as many prizes as possible that we could raffle and auction on the night. As with the email for the radio stations, I thought, *Well, it worked before; there is no reason it won't work again.*

I emailed many organisations, including both Liverpool and Everton football clubs, not really expecting to get a response, never mind a prize, but to my amazement, both clubs sent prizes with a good luck message, along with signed gloves from boxer David Price. When you are determined to make a success of something as well as make a difference in the world, nothing will stand in your way. With the big

36

names such as David Price and both football clubs, other prizes were donated, including a night in a top hotel, spa packages, and hair and beauty packages. This was all done in the space of six weeks, proving what can be done when you are determined. I was able to raise much needed funds for two very worthy charities on the night of the launch, benefitting those less fortunate.

That interview was to be the first of many I have conducted, not just in Merseyside, but also a couple in New York and one in London, as well as TV shows and an article in the local paper through the support and guidance from a women's organisation I belong to.

This organisation offers services to help women set up in business; they not only featured my business on the launch of their new business club, they also mentioned it in an article in the *Liverpool Echo*. Having no funds available for advertising my book and my business could have presented an obstacle to stop me, but I ensured with determination I would make it a success. After the interview with Pete Price and the launch, I was then invited into the studios of Radio Merseyside to conduct an interview with Sean Styles; the two radio stations brought untold success to the sales of the book. These two radio stations had played a huge part in my childhood, and they were now playing a major role in the promotion of my first book. I could not have been more thrilled; this was a huge accolade for me. With these interviews now under my belt, I felt there was nothing I couldn't accomplish.

I then decided I might as well keep knocking on doors; so many had opened for me, there was no reason I could not continue this luck and really go all out. If I had made radio, why shouldn't I try TV? I had a six-month plan to promote my book, and in October I attended a woman's event in Bristol and decided to email Bay TV, which covers the whole of Merseyside and Cheshire, reaching an audience of just under one million. I was really aiming high now, trying to get on TV, but I have always believed unless you try, you will never know what results you will get. I sent the email at 9.30 one night whilst sitting in my hotel room, not really expecting a reply, but the next morning at ten o'clock., I received a reply from Neil Duffin, informing me they would love to interview me.

I was now displaying every kind of emotion you can think of, from excitement to amazement and then sheer panic that I was actually going to be interviewed on TV less than twenty-four hours after sending in my request. I was now going to get my story out on local TV.

To be totally honest, I really didn't expect a reply, and that was the reason for the panic. I hadn't really thought about what I would do in a TV interview. Yes, I had been on radio, but this was a whole new ballgame, although in all of it, I had proven once again, no matter what the situation, anything is possible with determination. As before, I was extremely nervous at the thought, but also very excited to learn a new skill. I was also excited about what was to come from the interview.

The interview took place in November and was aired on 15 December; it was also on YouTube. The interview was very relaxed and took place in Central Library in Liverpool; it felt like a friendly chat between two friends. If someone would have told me the level of promotion my book would get without any funds, I would have thought they were crazy.

Now I had been on TV and radio, and four months had gone by; how was I going to continue with the exposure I wanted for the book? After my interview with Bay TV, I decided I would now target libraries and generate interest in stocking the book. The support from local establishments was huge when it came to local talent being promoted; after getting my book in the libraries, I had this yearning inside to market to audiences I hadn't yet reached, so I then decided to write to another Mersey radio station I had found via the Internet. For me to get the coverage and the word out about my book, I had to ensure I continually looked for ways to promote it. There was no better way than via radio and TV, so Mersey Radio was definitely another great stage to showcase *Opening Doors*.

I knew, just as the previous radio stations, it reaches an audience across the globe, so continuing with the media campaign would give me the best chance of success for the book. Again to my surprise, Jason Pinnington, the show's producer, wrote back to advise me they were interested in conducting an interview with me on 4 January. Local historian Frank Carlyle would be the interviewer; strangely enough, he had grown up in the same area as my mum and was actually friends with my uncles. By now, my confidence after having a number of interviews was at an all-time high; this interview felt very different from the previous ones, which had taught me how to prepare and what the listeners wanted to hear. I was now growing to a level that would have been a dream eighteen months before.

It comes naturally to me to keep challenging myself, but I had proven to myself over and over again what can be achieved. When I had left my job the year before, I could never have imagined the journey I would go on, but I used all these keys to unlock the doors put in front of me.

What does determination look like to you? How would you define it? I would say it is a drive inside that pushes you forward; it comes from your soul, telling you whatever you want to accomplish is right there in front of you if you want it enough. Determination is built from the inside out; mine has shown itself in every aspect of my life whenever there has been a challenge I had to overcome. If you look deep within, you will find yours; you may have to dig a little deeper, but it is there.

Determination can also be associated with resilience and how well you rise after falling, rather than giving up at the first hurdle. If you keep trying, you may be surprised at how far you can go. By never giving up, you are building determination from within to always reach for more; perseverance and persistence are also strongly linked with it. If you can build each of these traits into your character, you have a better chance of achieving your goals.

KEY 6

Action

It is all well and good to build on all the previous skills, but they will amount to nothing if you don't have my next key. I would not have come as far as I have if I didn't have this key. No matter how strong my vision was, how determined I was, or how my confidence and self-belief had grown, without this key, my book would have been gathering dust on bookstore shelves and generating no interest on Amazon and the other websites it was being sold on. It was paramount I had this within me if this book was going to have the impact I wanted it to have. I wanted my story to be the one that helped others make the changes they had always wanted in their lives, and if I was going to do that, there was one more key I definitely needed to open up those locked doors, and that key is action.

If we are to achieve our dream, we must have the action within us to make it happen, so it was important I have this in abundance. What do I mean when I talk about having action within you?

When we are chasing results, no matter what those results are, we must have action within us to keep going, even when we come up against a brick wall or hear the voices of critics telling us it can't be done. The person I will use as an example in this chapter is an individual I have used quite a lot within my book. The reason for that is he displays a number of the keys discussed in this book. Thomas Edison is a prime example; no matter how many times he failed, he still had action within him to keep going. When we are faced with obstacles in our quest to achieve our goals, it is so easy to give up, but when you are as determined as this man was, you will find that action inside to keep searching. No matter how many times we fail at something, if we believe, then we will keep pushing ahead.

My desire to succeed as a coach and speaker pushed me forward, ensuring I had action within me to keep going. My passion for helping others fulfil their dreams and achieve their goals was enough to make me take action. Actions speak louder than words, and when we act out what we want, we show the world how we are going to achieve it.

The opposite of taking action, procrastination, can have a huge impact on us and our dreams. No matter what other skills we possess, without action, those skills will amount to nothing. They won't get you to your destination, so remember, when you procrastinate, that means you are not taking the action needed to fulfil your desires.

In order to accomplish any task, whether that is in our personal life or in business, we must always be active to get the result we want. Whenever we take action, we are showing the world we are serious in our quest to achieve our dreams, which will also inspire others to do the same.

Here is an example of where action was taken: when Ebola was diagnosed, the government took action to stop the spread of the disease. Action within you will be stronger depending on what result you are chasing and why you want it; always ensure whatever you are working towards is crucial towards achieving your end goal, as this will determine how active you are.

KEY 7

Knowledge

For many successful individuals, key 7 is an important factor; it is crucial in my keys to success and something we all must continually build on to be successful in our chosen path. Whether you are studying at a university or starting a new company, knowledge is the most valuable tool you can work on to be the best version of yourself.

As we grow from children, this skill will take us into adulthood and further on, again by building on it right throughout our lives. It is something we do on a daily basis but don't really think about.

For every new path we may take in life, knowledge is something we must work on every day, by stretching ourselves to keep learning about whatever subject we care about. No one person has all the knowledge or the answers; we are all masters in our own fields, but you can be the go-to person by continually building on it. When you build knowledge, this also builds competence, and that then builds confidence, so just by increasing your knowledge, you are building skills you might not have realised you had.

Here is an example of how I built my knowledge. I was hired to manage the Blackburn branch; although other branches had issues that I needed to know about, Blackburn was one of the bigger branches and had very complex problems. To be successful, I had to know the problems the branch faced; this was of the highest importance so I could come up with solutions to those problems, but also to contribute to the company's bottom line profits and improve the branch's capabilities.

If we were to grow within the branch, I had to up-skill every single person who worked there, and that could only be done if I improved my knowledge about the branch.

For the eighteen months I was at Blackburn, the success we had would not have happened had I not continually worked on my knowledge of not only the issues within the branch as well as the staff, but also the environment and the customers. By understanding all the needs and continually educating myself on the complexity of the branch, I ensured that improvements would happen. And if that meant working late into the night, analysing trends and data, then so be it. My work didn't end when I left the office. I was determined to turn this branch around and have it rise from the ashes, so I regularly worked until the small hours building my knowledge. If I hadn't done this, we would have gotten very different results.

Momentum in learning and building up your knowledge will take you to the next level in your quest to achieve the results you desire. Momentum only happens when you do something regularly; this guarantees you keep moving forward. If I didn't have momentum in building up my knowledge, then the results in Blackburn would not have come, and further success I achieved in my career at the company would not have happened. Do whatever it takes to build up your knowledge: read books, get advice from others who have been there before you, shadow people who are doing the job you want, or get a mentor who can teach you the skills you need. You can also educate yourself by attending courses that will help you retain the knowledge you need in your new path.

Since embarking on my new career, I had to retrain and educate myself to the highest standard and build my knowledge in whatever subjects I would be coaching others in. I had built up certain skills in leadership, sales, and coaching, but I wasn't actually certified (although I do believe it takes more than a piece of paper to prove you can do a job). Experience on the job is always the best form of learning for me. That said, I decided I needed to up-skill myself to guarantee results for my future clients.

If I was to help them become the best version of themselves, I had to be the best version of me and have the knowledge of each subject required to make them want to choose me as their coach.

By joining organisations that are known for their expertise, I was ensuring I was at the top of my game when it came to knowledge. I was open to different ways of learning and growing as a coach and public speaker, continually developing my skills, which I could then pass onto my clients with confidence. After meeting a guy called Billal Jamil at an event in London in February 2015 I became a member of the Public Speaking Academy and also had one two one coaching sessions with Billal, this man gave me the courage and the confidence to never be afraid to reach for heights I had never reached before. they say if your dreams don't scare you they aren't big enough, well mine have always gone way beyond what others would believe possible and with Billal's guidance and coaching I achieved everything and more. I now pass on his coaching methods to my own clients supporting them to achieve the ultimate.

In any profession, knowledge is the key to how you will perform; the better your knowledge, the bigger the result you will achieve. Whether you are a cleaner or the director of a company, the level of knowledge in your field will define what your outcome will be. The same is true for a policeman and a doctor; a policeman cannot recite the law unless he has studied and learnt it word for word, and doctors cannot treat a patient with the right medication if they have not learnt about the patient's medical history. They can do this by learning what tools to put in place to help their knowledge grow. This is the reason for medical charts; they are building up a picture of a patient's health and this can mean the difference between life and death.

Imagine the consequences if employees in a big company like Virgin or Jaguar were not up to speed with new information and it impacted the services these companies provide; this would not only affect bottom line profits but also the reputation of the company, damaging future sales. Future employees would not want to be associated with a company that is not training or developing its staff.

Cars are a massive commodity in today's society, and the big car companies like Jaguar, Audi, and Ford are looking to build the next big car that will bring huge profits. The average household has two cars on the path. In January 2015, there were 26.7 million households in the UK; the car industry would be destroyed if employees were not continually working on their knowledge skills.

Knowledge will always play a huge part in my journey. In all organisations, it is important for all employees to build on their knowledge; this is a crucial component to a business's objectives and success.

KEY 8

Goal-Setting

My eighth key probably ensured I would be successful in whatever I did. This is the key that kept my dreams alive from a tiny little girl who grew up very poor. I made a decision from a very young age: my own children would not be born into poverty. That all important key is goal-setting. When I first started writing my goals down, I was just writing out my wishes. I was so young, I didn't understand how important this skill was and how it would impact my life so much in the years ahead. By writing my goals down, I was visualising and believing I would achieve the things I desired.

I knew as a family we did not have the spare cash for the luxuries some of my friends had, so I had to find a way of achieving them as I got older. Looking back, the first goal I set myself was when my eldest sister taught me how to tell the time; I must have been around three, and she would sit me on her knee each day and get me to recite what she had taught me the day before. Each night, I would take the clock to bed and practice, preparing myself for what she would do the next day. I would set myself a target of learning the minutes and the hours as well as what past and to meant. This seemed to work; I didn't know this then, but what I was really doing was forming the skills to set and achieve regular goals whenever I wanted to accomplish something.

When I recall doing this from a child, I am unsure of where I learnt this. I am certain it came from the desperation to improve my life. As I got older and my dreams and desires got bigger, I would form a plan of how I would achieve them. A goal written down is only a dream unless you have action within you of how you are moving forward.

As a little girl, I would often get lost in a programme called *Black Beauty*, my imagination would run wild of how life could be with the desire and determination within you. I would regularly write down everything I wanted to achieve and visualise achieving it; this would give me the fire inside to do whatever was possible to make it happen. For me, the biggest goal I ever achieved as a child was shopping in Next, a store I was so desperate to shop in. At the age of fourteen, I had written down that I would spend my first week's salary in this store after I got a job. I had regularly envisioned going into this shop and kept that vision clear in my mind. When it was getting closer to leaving school, I looked for jobs that would help me realise my dream, and that dream became reality when I started work in a printers. My salary was £57 per week; this was more than enough for me to buy a suit from Next. This is when I realised how important it was to always write your goals down.

Everyone has the desire to dream big and the ability to live out those dreams. We desire to improve our own lives and also our family's, but can we all follow through? Yes, we can, if we really want it enough. You just need courage and inspiration, which can change your life for the better.

Everyone has it inside to not only dream of a better life but also to pursue one, and each of us have the cognitive ability to set out our plans strategically on how we will accomplish it. First of all, you have to know what your end goal is; this is so important when writing down your goals.

Each time I set myself a new goal, I always know what I want the end to look like; that way, I know what I am working towards. I then have to work out how I will get there. I look at what I have already done so far; from this, I can then decide what my next step will be.

All of us have a dream we want to achieve; for some, it may be the top of the list. Others may have buried them deep inside; they may not believe they are worthy of them due to listening to others around them.

When you think about what excites you or wakes you up through the night, it's usually what you dream of. How would you feel if you accomplished it? What could you do when you have achieved it? What would you try if you were guaranteed to succeed? When you have the answers to these questions, you will then know what your biggest goal is, and that is when your plan starts coming together and you start to strategically set out to achieve it.

I have set numerous goals for myself over the years; I start by finding out why it is important to me. Your "why" is the biggest drive to keep you moving closer to achieving it. This will determine how hard you work towards it, helping you to prioritise how you are going to get there, what you will need to do, who can help you, and how long it will take you to accomplish it. You can also look at who has been there before you and what you can learn from them.

Goals need to be smart as well as realistic; smart goals must be specific, measurable, attainable, realistic, and time bound if you are to succeed.

Within my personal life and career, there have been many goals I have been proud of. Two of them will always stand out for me. The first one is very personal to me: when we bought our first home. Everything was stacked against us when we first looked at this house, but I had set myself the goal of owning it, and nothing could stand in my way. Over the years when I have been very close to walking away from a challenging situation, the memories of the day I received the keys to our first home and the feeling inside always push me forward.

When I achieve a goal, I then set myself a new one. I am continually growing, developing, and learning new ways of working. The other goal that stands out was probably way out of my comfort zone, but they do say for us to grow to our highest level, comfort zones are not the place to be. I decided to take the bull by the horns and completely throw caution to the wind with this one. I knew if I overcame this, then the impossible would become the possible.

If I was to become a motivational speaker people wanted to listen to, and be able to engage with my audience, I had to do something extraordinary. Setting this goal for myself would take me to a place I had never been before; it also terrified the life out of me. I knew how much I wanted to be a speaker and a coach, and doing this would definitely help me build up rapport with my audience: I would become a stand-up comic.

After writing my first book, I decided to research comedy courses, not really believing at the time I would complete one. I was just looking to see what options were available, and I found one with the Liverpool Comedy Festival. For six weeks, I would learn the ropes of stand-up comedy. I knew if I could master this, then speaking about subjects I knew and understood would be a lot easier. Well, that first night, I was not even able to stand up for thirty seconds, but six weeks later, I delivered a nine-minute routine in front of over two hundred people. I really had achieved the impossible.

When I attended that first night, I really was at my lowest; just getting through the night was a miracle, and I thought it would be my last, after the shock of finding out I had to perform in front of family and friends six weeks down the line. I never really thought I would even find a course, let alone write my own material. So as you can see, when we are serious about achieving our goals, nothing can stop us. When we are living our most purposeful lives and doing what we were put on this earth for, miracles happen, and doors open of their own accord. It was no coincidence that I found the course that would take me to my next chapter on my journey. What we send out will always come back, and by writing my goals down to build up my confidence and complete a comedy course, the universe was listening and gave me what I was asking for. I was on the path I was always meant to be on, and just like all the previous coincidences that had happened, this was no accident.

The reaction I received after the gig still amazes me. I had no intention of ever becoming a stand-up comic; that course was for one thing, and one thing only: to help build up my confidence. After I went on stage, the gig was uploaded to YouTube and has had over one thousand hits.

From writing a goal to find a comedy course to now having my gig on YouTube, I could not comprehend it, but this shows what can happen if you really do want to meet your goals.

I regularly read famous quotes from people who have been there and done it before us, this is what continually spurs me on to keep writing my goals down.

Jim Rohn: "If you don't design your own life plan, chances are you'll fall into someone else's plan. And guess what they have planned for you? Not much."

Orison Swett Marden: "All who have accomplished great things have had a great aim, have fixed their gaze on a goal which was high, one which sometimes seemed impossible."

Og Mandino: "I am here for a purpose and that purpose is to grow into a mountain, not to shrink to a grain of sand, henceforth will I apply my efforts to become the highest mountain of all, and I will strain my potential until it cries for mercy."

These are just a few quotes about goal-setting, which plays a huge part in my life. Little did I know when I set my very first goal at the tender age of three how important a skill that was. I believe I have come this far because I learned it so early. Although goal-setting can be learned at any time, the earlier you learn, the easier it is to set them. They say when you do something for twenty-one days, it becomes a habit. Make it a positive one and start writing your goals down. Remember to break them down into little chunks and also set short-, medium-, and long-term goals; by doing this, you are setting yourself up for success. Goal-setting works in both our personal and business lives, and I believe is very important to your future growth. By setting regular goals and achieving them, you will be building a skill which will impact every area of your life.

KEY 9

Passion

The ninth key I used in my quest to realise my dreams is passion. This is ultra-important in determining whether you succeed or not. I had this in abundance when growing up as a little girl. I remember my old headmistress in junior school telling me I wouldn't amount to much; I can still picture myself looking at her and thinking, *I may never be a teacher, but whatever I become, I will be great at it because of my passion.* I was only around ten at the time; when you have passion, it is clear to see.

The passion I always carried came from my own mum. I watched from a very young age how her passion was evident in everything she did. I took this trait from her and applied it to every single task I have undertaken.

Passion is that strong emotion within us when we embark on a new venture; it defines how well we do, whether we perform at our highest level or are mediocre in what we achieve.

In my first book, I wrote about my passion for people and how important that is for anything we do in life. When we build strong, compassionate relationships, we are already successful. I believe people are at the heart of every bit of success we acquire. In our lives, there will be other factors that push us to continue to achieve; for instance, people wishing for us to fail can also push us forward to continue to achieve, but this will only keep us focused for so long. It is always our passion that forms how well we do.

When you link passion to purpose, you will live, breathe, and sleep it. Some people may consider you crazy, that is what passion does for you, and that is why this key is very important on your journey to discovery. The more passion you carry for whatever you are chasing, the bigger the result will be.

When I am passionate about a task, I can become quite obsessed. I will live, breathe, and sleep it; every waking moment will be spent on the project at hand. Passion is not something you can touch or feel in a physical form; it is an effect of what you do.

Passion will ensure you keep getting back up, no matter how many times you fall. It is also something that will turn thoughts into reality, even when you believe there is nothing left to give. It's that feeling deep in the pit of your stomach where if you reach in with your hand, you can touch it. Passion will also have you working voluntarily; this is when your passion is linked with your purpose, because it is important to follow through, whether it is paid or unpaid. You will do whatever it takes to get results; your passion is also something you can't switch off. It is always there at the front of your mind.

It could be a promotion from your current position, a complete change in your career, or even defining your own destiny and taking charge of your own life. Passion is closely associated with drive, energy, and enthusiasm; motivation will be uplifted at the thought of what you want to achieve.

People who display passion are usually very ambitious and have high aspirations. Passion is about being brave enough to acknowledge and embrace these expectations. I am a very passionate person and will always challenge the status quo if it is something that I feel is not right or if it affects others. I regularly push boundaries and ultimately want to reshape the world.

When you strive to be passionate about something, you have to be prepared to stand out for the right reasons and not be just another face in the crowd.

Here is an example of how I display passion and what it means to me: although I am passionate about a lot of work I have undertaken, nothing is more important than charity work. When you are giving back, whether that be money or time, this is the greatest gift you can give to someone.

I was passionate about getting my first book published, and inspiring others to believe the impossible can become the possible is what fuelled my desire to ensure it was completed within one year. There may be many reasons why you want to achieve something. I had a number of reasons for ensuring my goals were met; I wanted to prove to certain individuals that they initially fuelled my desire to succeed, but it was my passion to keep achieving and pushing myself that kept the momentum up.

I have always been passionate about getting results, and when I set myself a goal, there is nothing that will stand in my way. Getting my book published in one year and reaching the largest possible audience was always going to be my biggest dream. If I was to inspire others to change their lives, then I had to ensure it went further than a dream. Writing the book was always going to be the easy part, as I knew my story by heart, but I was not familiar with marketing and promoting. There were times I recall wondering why this was so important to me and why I needed to get this story out, and the same answer would continually go around in my head.

There are people across the world who have been dealt a hand like the one I had been dealt, in both my personal and my career. I had worked for a company for over twenty years and thought it would continue to play a huge part in my life even into retirement. I had a lot of love for it, and then in 2012, that all changed, and my life went on a downward spiral for two years. I was left with no choice but to resign for the sake of my health; before then, if I went to the doctors a couple times in a year, that was a lot. I was at such a dark place in my life, the doctor's was my second home. Everything I had ever known was slowly disappearing in front of me; my passion not just for work but life in general was also gone, and I was finding it difficult to put one foot in front of the other. That happy-go-lucky person I had always been was replaced by a paranoid and nervous wreck who couldn't even think straight. Knowing that others were playing a big part in that change was very difficult for me to swallow.

I had given my best years to this company, and now here I was, on the verge of a breakdown, and my passion to fight back and stand up for what I believed in was all but gone. The only option for me was to resign from the job I loved, and as difficult as it was, it was a decision that had to be made if I wanted to get my sanity back.

When you are driven to the depths of despair, there is only one way to go, and that is back up. I was going back up, alright; I knew that passionate person was still there, somewhere deep inside. If I searched enough, I would one day find her again. And that day came on 10 July 2014, when I decided to write *Opening Doors*. If this book was to help me find me again, then I had to ensure I had a good story to tell and encourage others to make the changes they want to see.

That is when my passion came back; a fire grew inside me to rise from the ashes and come back tenfold. My passion was now written so big, in my mind, that I could not give up until the book was written and accessible right across the world. The only way I could achieve that was through a huge marketing and promotional campaign. This was a path I had never been down before, so it was all new to me. How would I get in front of the right people? Who would I need to speak to? How would I even create a media campaign with no money? I wrote these questions down and continually stared at the paper, with no real answers, and then all of a sudden, the solution started to form in my mind. I drafted an email to media organisations and sent it off to them, not sure if I would get a reply. I then decided to build a social media presence by joining the platforms where I thought I had the best chance of showcasing my book. I started to write blogs and build up a following with my work. I wanted to give others something they could take away and use, and from this desire came the ultimate: I was contacted by Jeffrey Hayzlett from C-Suite Network, enquiring if I would appear on his show in New York. Now this was yet another level; yes, I had been on radio and local TV, but we are talking American TV here. I am still not sure how it happened, but it did. This adventure I was now on was not only going to be educating me, it was also going to be amazing.

As part of my campaign, I had tried my hand with Loose Women and was unsuccessful; although I still haven't given up on that, I learned from other strong women, and they are some of the strongest women on UK TV.

Being offered an opportunity like this was terrifying but also exciting, and one I wasn't passing up; the title of my first book is *Opening Doors*; I believe behind every new door is a new opportunity for us to learn and develop as well as evolve, and that is exactly what this was for me. My book has really gone international, and now I have a second book to launch and conduct interviews for. This truly is what dreams are made of and proof of what can happen when your dreams become reality.

So my passion for succeeding is what pulled me back from a mental breakdown and pushed me to not only write a book but also learn new skills along the way. Because I was not able to pay for publicity for the book, I was able to learn and become a promoter and marketer, proving once again how far we can really go when we believe.

I would say to anyone who is faced with difficult times in their lives, when you reach down, that passion to keep fighting is there; you sometimes have to go places you have never been before, but if you are willing, you will find it.

The passion I carry will always keep me interested in and focused on the task at hand, ensuring I will always succeed at whatever I set myself. Ensure you link your passion to your purpose; this is what will keep you moving forward. If you hit a brick wall, somehow you will smash through, even when the odds are stacked against you.

KEY 10

Success

My final key is one that everyone defines differently. it also forms part of the title for the book. Success is my final key. I believe it cements all the keys together to form one master key, bringing me success in all areas of my life, including spiritually.

When we are faced with difficult times in our lives, there are a number of ways we can be pulled. After being faced with a mental breakdown and not understanding how I got there, I was searching for answers as to why people do things that can affect others so badly that they consider the best option is suicide. I found a book that I recommend for anyone looking to grow spiritually; that book is called *The Monk Who Sold His Ferrari* by Robin Sharma. This book gave me the answers I had been looking for and helped me on my journey to recovery. I would recommend it for anyone who wants to develop spiritually.

Exceptionally successful people share a number of traits that help them on their path to success. Success only comes through your action to achieve your goals; it encourages you to continually strive for more. It also means different things to different people. Individuals define success in a number of areas; what they have accomplished throughout their lives is always a deciding factor in whether they believe they have been successful.

I regularly get asked the same questions: how did I become successful, and what did I do differently from the next person? Over the years, my answer has been different; as an individual, I have changed and evolved from the child I was to the woman I have become, and I will continue to change as the years go on.

Growing up very poor, I could have seen success as acquiring and owning material goods; I could have gone through the years that way, but bringing my own children into the world changed how I saw success in a big way. I realised it is not the amount of material things you have or the amount of money you earn; it is about the amount of lives you can change as well as the impact you have on the world. Brendan Burchard has a quote I have come to live by: "When we are at the end of our earthly life, there are three questions we should ask ourselves: 'Did I live? Did I love? Did I matter?'" This quote sums up how we will all feel at the end. I happen to mention it twice in the book, and the reason for that is the impact those words have had on me as an individual.

Tony Robbins says that success without fulfilment is failure; he interviewed numerous clients for his last book, *Money: Master the Game*, and in that book, he describes how some of them had everything in terms of money and material things but were still unhappy. Why? Because they didn't have fulfilment.

Look at Robin Williams, who had everything; anything he turned his hand to, he made a success of it, even winning an award for a serious role. He decided he wanted to take on a dramatic role and give something else to the world; he achieved this and won an Academy Award, but again all the money, fame, and awards were not enough to fill that gap inside, and in August 2014, the world lost a great man when he took his life. Success does not always mean fulfilment,

Robbins also states we need to master both achievement and fulfilment; how do we do this? First, we must be passionate about what we are pursuing (whether that is personal or business). If we are not passionate about the goal we are chasing, it will not be achieved. For change to happen in any of the above, it is important that we display that passion as we regularly move forward in pursuit of our dreams. More importantly, you need to know your "why," as this is what will keep you focused when you are finding walls closing in on you and results aren't coming. When you know your why, it will not only wake you up through the night, it will also get you out of bed in the morning, excited to start the day ahead, working towards accomplishing your dream.

Hunger is what differentiates those who achieve success from those that don't. How hungry are you? Ask yourself what else you can do that will move you closer; what have you not done yet that will make the difference? These are two questions I regularly ask myself when I come up against obstacles.

In addition to fulfilment, I consider gratitude an extremely important part of success. This goes hand-in-hand with fulfilment; when you display gratitude in your life, this then sends out a message to the universe, opening up further opportunities that may come your way.

I grew up in a very poor family. I have been very lucky to have achieved the success I have, as well as provide a comfortable life for my children, so I continually show my gratitude by giving back. It may only be a smile to someone who is having a bad day or an "Hello, how is your day going?" By taking the time to do this, imagine the impact you can have on someone who is having the worst day possible. It really can make a huge difference. Or it could be taking the time to sit and talk to a homeless person; it is not always about giving them money. For me, personally, I think it is easy to just give them money; if you take the time to ask them how they are or what brought them to this point in their life, it could even trigger something inside them to find a solution and improve their situation.

Sometimes, people don't know why they have a problem until they are questioned. Success to a homeless person would be finding shelter for the night, somewhere dry to sleep, as well as a hot meal and drink; that same person could also make a difference in someone else's life, if they are given the chance, and by you taking the time to talk with them, it could give them the encouragement and confidence to do something about it. And even if they don't change, at least you made their day a little brighter by taking the time to talk to them.

I myself have watched how many people walk past the homeless; I often wondered what sort of life they led. Are they happy? Do they have issues so bad in their own lives that they don't feel like they can help someone else, or are they just ignorant to what is going on around them? Whatever it may be, they are entitled to have those reasons, although I find when we give instead of just taking, that is the start to feeling fulfilled.

In my first book, I wrote about how I always wanted to help others, and this still continues today. I believe we are all put on this earth for a purpose, and when you discover that purpose, that is the day you truly start living. I have encountered many obstacles and challenges in my life, but they ensured I was fully equipped to help others who are facing similar challenges.

My first book did not start out as a book; it began when I wrote my thoughts down after the worst two years of my life. My intention when writing was to simply get over what had happened; up until then, I had woken up every day grateful for everything I had achieved in my career. I was having a life that, as a child, would have been nothing more than a dream, but I had worked damn hard to accomplish what I had. I had worked my way up from grassroots level to a senior position, continually educating myself along the way. I didn't only want success for myself, I also wanted it for those who worked under my leadership.

The company had given me a foundation on which I was growing on a daily basis, so when I decided to resign, it wasn't a decision I was making faint-heartedly. It could also have worked out very differently if I didn't have that hunger inside to keep going. No matter what you face, with action and determination, there are no limits to what you can achieve. Although the company had given me a foundation, and I will always be grateful, I had given them a whole lot more. I was regularly asked to go into underperforming branches to turn them around, and not once did I refuse. I not only wanted to keep learning new skills, by going into these locations and turning them into top-performing branches, I also wanted to encourage others to achieve more. I set an example, by the actions I took and the strategies I put in place, to help them improve their own abilities. All that I had learned from a self-employed agent through to area manager brought me continued success. I could relate to each of the people who worked for me, and more often than not, I had a solution for every problem they encountered, and if I didn't, I would research or find someone who did have the answer.

When you have put your heart and soul into a project and every waking moment is spent living it, you don't expect it to be taken away from you, but sure enough, it was.

The people now working in the company were very different from what I knew; they were not sitting with the values and morals I carried from a little girl. Only two months before I stopped enjoying my job, I had sat at the boardroom table with a number of other area managers as well as the CEO and directors, discussing tactics and strategies on how to improve results within the company. I cannot comprehend how my life and attitude had changed in such a short space of time. I would not have expected the dramatic change to happen so quickly, but it did, and over those two years, I had to dig deep to understand the actions of others. I have to say I haven't always found the answers; however, it did teach me that when we are forced in directions we wouldn't normally have gone, there is only one way, and that is up.

As I was writing my thoughts down, I realised I am not the only person who faces these challenges, and by publishing it, it could actually make a difference to so many lives and also help others find the path they were always meant to be on. Sometimes, we are forced in directions we ought to have found ourselves, so being forced in a direction is God's way of placing us where we should be.

I view every trial or tribulation I face as a new opportunity; by doing this, you are creating a new beginning. When you are faced with this, always remember that you can change your life for the better.

I would never have imagined leaving the role I had worked so hard for, but it was forced upon me. I was left with no choice other than to resign and pursue whatever adventure awaited me. I have always believed life is one big adventure and we must learn something new every day, so I took this as a chance to learn new skills, which I could pass on and teach others and, at the same time, enjoy and embrace them. When you can adapt to change, it will enrich your life in more ways than you can imagine.

This was a huge change, as my whole career had been built on this company, and leaving to start something new scared the hell out of me. As they say a change is as good as a rest and that was how I would view this.

Was I angry? Of course I was, but I was not going to carry that anger, because that would have impeded my success moving forward. Do people know (or care) that you are angry with them? No, they don't;

when you carry anger, you only hurt yourself. I had to get rid of the anger I was carrying and turn it into excitement to be starting a new chapter in my life. Life is one big book in which there are different chapters, and this was a new one that awaited me.

I always knew I would succeed; as I stated earlier, successful people share certain traits. It was up to me to now create the success I had previously had, only this time, rather than benefitting those I don't believe deserved it, I would get to choose who I wanted to benefit from it.

A leader to me is someone who trusts their people, believes in their people, encourages them, and supports them along the way. This was no longer happening in the company; when that respect has gone, it is time to move on, for both yourself and the company. It did take a lot of soul-searching over the two years; was it a phase or was it me as person? Was I no longer enjoying the role or had I surpassed it? These were questions I asked myself over that time, along with what I thought success was.

Before September 2012, I had considered success to be earning a good salary and ensuring the happiness of my family, as well as giving when I could, but no amount of money could bring me success if I was unhappy in my role, and that is when the decision became easy.

In the two years since my resignation, you could say the level of success I have achieved from getting my first book published to now finishing my second one and preparing for TV interviews and another book launch is up there with the best. Of course, that is success.

What I consider more successful is rising after falling so hard and contemplating suicide to now making a difference in others' lives through the work I now do.

I have met fantastic business leaders who have taught me how to make a success of a business, but they also make it their life's work to help others. Through the new path I have found myself on, I have met a woman called Jean Taylor, who is a beacon of light in others' lives. This for me is what success stands for.

Yes, I may have been very successful in my previous role, but did I add value besides teaching them new skills? I am not sure I did. I may have coached and developed them, but did I change their mind-sets to look at life in a very different way? No, I don't think I did. Maybe I had to go through what I did in those two years to learn the true value of success.

When I look back over that time, I am now grateful for everything that happened, as I would not be the person I am today. I am also a whole lot richer for the people I have met whilst on this journey I call my adventure of life. When you are inspiring others to go out and believe in their dreams, and they go out and achieve them, that is what true success means to me.

I have used these ten keys throughout my life to bring me continued success; they may not be what you need to bring you your own success, but they may give you an idea of what you can do differently to achieve the ultimate: to be the person you were put on this earth for.

Personal development is massive, right across the world today, and for anyone wanting to see changes in their lives, it is important they embrace it. I had worked in the corporate world and attended numerous workshops and courses to sustain the level of results I was getting, but I had to leave and find my own path to not just learn new ways of learning but also how to develop further as a person and get the most out of myself.

Tony Robbins, Oprah Winfrey, and Richard Branson all had similar (if not worse) childhoods than me, and they have still gone out and achieved success. I believe success is there for anyone, but it doesn't come easy. You have to have action within you and a never-say-never attitude, as well as that hunger to keep going and the determination inside to keep searching for new ways to succeed.

When you have all of the above traits, it is only a matter of time before your big break comes, and people will be looking to you for guidance and advice. I have a quote I live by, and it drives me every day: "There is a time for everything, but how does one recognise the time to leave or the time to open new doors?" Do you know if it is that time in your life when you should close the doors that have held you back for so long and open the doors to a brighter future, one which will bring you success in every area of life?

Is there a change you would like to see happen, but you don't know how to make it? By following these ten keys, or searching inside yourself to find your own keys to success, you can achieve everything you have always wished for.

As well as everything else I have achieved in the previous two years, in June of this year I was named ambassador for an international festival for business here in Liverpool, a business event which saw over one hundred countries and thirty thousand delegates involved, proving with the right mind-set and determination, our goals will always be met.

I will leave you with this thought: there are times in our lives that can define who we become; ensure you define who you become, and do not let the actions of others dictate it. Let their actions be the fuel inside that takes you to places you have never been before.

Remember, it is our own inner voice that we hear when we are looking to achieve our goals; let it be the voice of optimism, enthusiasm, and clarity. This is the voice that will serve you throughout life.

In the words of Gerry Marsden, "When you walk through a storm, hold your head up high and don't be afraid of the dark; at the end of the storm, there's a golden sky and the sweet silver song of the lark."

Walk on.

Lightning Source UK Ltd.
Milton Keynes UK
UKOW03f0141090217
293936UK00001B/234/P